NEW BEGINNINGS

How God Delivered Me From Alcohol And Drugs!

REM007

Order this book online at www.trafford.com
or email orders@trafford.com

Most Trafford titles are also available at major online book retailers.

Life experience and GODLY intervention

Printed in the United States of America.

ISBN: 978-1-4269-5298-2 (sc)
ISBN: 978-1-4269-5299-9 (e)

Trafford rev. 12/16/2010

 www.trafford.com

North America & international
toll-free: 1 888 232 4444 (USA & Canada)
phone: 250 383 6864 ♦ fax: 812 355 4082

NEW BEGINNINGS

HOW GOD DELIVERED ME FROM ALCOHOL AND DRUGS!

She grabbed a bag and packed it as fast as she could. It was time for her and her two kids to leave. She was tired of being ridiculed for her mistakes. You would think that no one has ever made a mistake before. Gladys is my mother, and as soon as the divorce was complete she could not get out of Georgia fast enough. After making a call to her brother Anthony, she earned enough money cleaning houses to get out of 'Dodge'. In 1965 it could not have been an easy decision to pick up everything you own and leave the only place you've ever known. But that is exactly what Gladys Eady Moore did after being ridiculed for giving birth in 1962 to a child "whom she named" Roger. This is where my story begins.

My name is Roger and I'm not that much different from the average 45 year old African American. I grew up in the 1960's, when times in the country were not all that comfortable for African Americans. Willard (my older brother) and I were the only two children my mother had at that time. Although she was married to Mr. Booker T. Moore, my father was a

1

man named Henry Thomas. Nine months after my parent's short romp in the back seat of a Studebaker, I was born. In this present day and age we have become accustomed to seeing this type of situation all too often. But in the early 1960's it was frowned on with vigorous contempt, as if people were not allowed to make mistakes. Even as adults we realize that people make bad decisions from time to time.

My mother was having a very bad relationship with Booker T., and she would often talk about her problems to Mr. Henry Thomas. As it turned out, the State of Georgia's Mental Health Department determined that Booker T. was mentally disturbed. He was institutionalized just before my mother left Georgia. Although my mother committed adultery with my father I do not hold any contempt for him, because of his attempts to care for me when I was an infant. My mother told me that Henry Thomas and his mother would constantly attempt to take me home with them. They were very concerned with my well being. So as it stands I forgive my mother for what probably turned out to be one minute of weakness, because her so-called husband (Booker T. Moore) was not fulfilling his responsibility as a husband or as a man.

From what I was able to gather from my mother, Mr. Moore's mental condition had been growing worse all the time he was in the relationship with her. Apparently something traumatic occurred to him in his childhood. My mother said her mother almost forced her to marry him because she was pregnant with my brother (Willard). I'm sure that she would not have married him if she could have left the area during her pregnancy. But then I would not be here to tell my story, because while my mother was pregnant with Willard, I was not yet conceived. Willard is three years older than I am, and he's very light skinned with gray eyes. As a matter of fact he looks just like his father. I've always had a feeling deep down on the inside that something was wrong, because I do not resemble my brother at all. When I look in the mirror my skin tone is different and my eye color is different as well, so I've always felt that something wasn't quite right with our father situation.

In the early years of my mother's life she found it difficult to get along with her siblings. From what I have been able to determine, Momma was treated like Cinderella, and the evil stepsister was her identical twin, my aunt Alicia. Alicia was recognized as the prettier of the two, and my mother said that Alicia was treated better than she was by their mother. My mother once told me of a situation where Alicia got a bad grade in school and my mother was yelled at, because of her sister's bad grade. When she told me that I found it hard to believe. How could someone be so mean? But as time went on I started to notice that my mother was a little mean herself, so then I started to believe her stories about her mother.

My Grandmother Trudy Eady was a sharecropper who gave birth to 8 children (Charlie, Antonio, Clinton, George, Momma, Alicia, Trudy Kate, and Laura). When my mother was born most of her brothers were already out of the home. The older brothers joined the Army and were either overseas or in a military base somewhere.

My mother was never very specific when she discussed the whereabouts of her brothers, so I never bothered to ask very many questions. But from what I understand no one wanted to stay around Grandma and Granddad very long. I think it was because of their strict rules. It could have very well been because of the fact that they lived in the back woods of Georgia where there was very little contact with other human beings.

I'm sure that it was uncomfortable being in a home with a mother who was constantly telling her how much trouble she was. Even though my mother was married and living with her husband and his mother, Momma found herself at home with her mother and father more often than not. She would ask her mother to babysit for her while she cleaned houses in an attempt to earn a living. The combined problems with Willard's father and her own mother caused my Momma to leave Georgia. I think that it was time for her to leave anyway. My mother once told me, "When I could no longer take orders from her and I thought I was grown, to the degree that I wanted to make my own decisions, then it was time for me to go." I think this is where she found herself in her own situation. She was no longer willing to listen to her mother or her so-called husband, so it was time for her to get out on her own. She had also made some mistakes and living in the area had to be very uncomfortable. Momma needed a NEW BEGINNING.

Upon arriving in Michigan, we went to my Uncle Antonio Eady's house. He and his wife Marcia lived in a small house in Detroit. They had two children named Mildred and Caroline. Uncle Antonio moved to Michigan after he was discharged from the Army. He was in the Korean War. After being discharged, he came to Detroit to pursue employment. He was hired by Ford Motor Company where he worked on the assembly line for 30 years. Uncle Antonio was an alcoholic. He and his brothers were involved with making and drinking moonshine when they were young. I found this out during a visit to my grandparents' home after graduating high school. This way of life carried into my uncle Antonio's later years and it became a constant problem. The corn liquor they made in the woods was very strong and possibly poisonous, according to what I have read about how corn liquor is manufactured. Being in a war must have been traumatic and very damaging to his self-esteem and his mind. A man can't take another life and not be changed for the rest of his life. I'm not attempting to give him an excuse for drinking, but when you do not understand whose you are you can't possibly know whom you are.

My mother would watch Uncle Antonio and Aunt Marcia argue with each other everyday. Momma knew that she could not continue living here in this environment with her two children being subjected to this abuse. So she got a job working on Grosse Isle, a small island in the Downriver area of Michigan. The island is known for its large expensive homes and very rich residents. Mama worked as a maid, cleaning their houses. When that job did not work out, she took a job as a cook on Visger Road, at Homespun Restaurant. Visger Road is the main avenue that separates two cities, River Rouge and Ecorse. Think of it as a "T" shaped city area. On the top of the "T" is the City of Detroit, and on the right side of the stem is the City of River Rouge, and on the left side of the stem is the City of Ecorse. This is what is known as the Tri-city area. Visger Road is unique because of the number of African American owned businesses that are in the area. Momma met Arthur Lee Buckner while working there and he eventually became her husband. Momma said he came in the restaurant everyday when he got off work. Arthur Lee was employed at U.S. Gypsum, a factory that manufactured cement and cement products.

I think that he must have represented that strong stable individual that my Momma had always longed for since her father was so weak. I believe that my mom had a secret desire to meet a strong man, something she was not accustomed to seeing during the early years of her life. My grandfather was a very soft spoken and humble man. He always served his wife and honored her with his substance. If one did not know him one would think that he was a wimp. But I beg to differ with that assumption, quite to the contrary. I think that he had to be very strong to endure the hardships they faced with on a daily basis. I have never been able to understand how much strength it required to be a sharecropper and pick cotton. The LORD had to truly be with my grandparents.

In 1966 Gladys Eady married Arthur Lee and became Gladys (Eady) Buckner. My mom gave birth to five children in this relationship. Clifton, Christian, Cheri Lynn, Ernest and Mickey. It seemed as if she was having a baby every week for a while. Anyway, she loved this guy, even though he would beat her brains out every week. On payday, which was every Friday, he (Arthur Lee) would go out with his friends and get drunk. When he came home, mom would say something about it and that would set him off. We lived in a one-bedroom apartment. There were six children and two adults. There was Willard, Clifton, Christian, Cheri Lynn, and myself. Ernest was a very small infant at this time. I remember once while Arthur Lee was beating my mother I attempted to stop him. He took one arm and threw me across the room. Needless to say that was the last time I tried that. You see Arthur Lee was 6 feet 8 inches tall. He probably weighed about 230 pounds.

I was very small at this time so I don't remember a lot about the early days of her relationship with Arthur Lee. However I do remember living on Visger Road during the worse winter storm in the history of Michigan. The storm of 1967 was horrible. There was almost 8 feet of snow. I remember my mother and father boiling water on the stove and pouring it out the front door so that we could make a path in the snow. The snow was so high that when we opened the front door, we could not see anything but snow. From the top of the door to the bottom it was completely packed with snow. After boiling the water, my mother would open the door and toss it at what seemed to be a large mass of white ice. After a few tosses we could finally begin to see what was on the outside. Nothing! Nothing was moving. I think the whole city was frozen. I remember climbing through the hole in the snow. I was so small that I got on my knees and crawled through the hole.

I should not pretend that all of our times with my stepfather were bad. That would not be true. There were times when we had fun also. We always looked forward to Christmas. This is when my mother would make Christmas bags for everyone. Even if we did not get any toys, we were still happy because we got a bag filled with fruit, candy and nuts. I do not know where my mom came up with the idea, but it was a fantastic one. Food was very hard to come by most of the time. As a matter of fact we were actually hungry most days during the month. My mom made it with little or no food most of the time. I remember eating hot water biscuits and syrup a great deal of the time during my childhood. Sometimes we also had to eat cereal with water because there was no milk. Now you may say, "I thought Arthur Lee worked everyday". Well he did. I think that was probably what he and my mother argued about constantly. I believe that he had another woman that he gave his money to when he got paid.

I don't remember many arguments between Arthur Lee and mom while we lived on Visger Road. But as soon as we moved to River Rouge, the address was on Holford Street, the arguments and the drinking became obvious and continual. I remember many days when he and my mother would fight. I would sit in the corner of the room and cry. Most of the time, I guess I was crying because of sadness. It was surely painful to watch this. I was told while writing this book that I should try to explain how things felt so that the reader could get an understanding of just what I was going through. But I find it hard to explain the pain. I remember sitting on the couch and hearing his car come down the block. Often I would think to myself, "I wonder if he is drunk today? What if they start fighting again today"? I guess the psychologist would say that this was child abuse. Maybe it was, but in 1968 no one worried so much about child abuse. The most horrific part about my life at this time was that seven people were living in a one-bedroom apartment, and we could not even afford a loaf of bread to eat. This to me was more painful and more abusive than anything else was.

Arthur Lee had a friend named "green coat". I guess they called him this because of the long three-quarter length Army 'P' coat that he wore everywhere everyday. When I think about it now, I think that he must have been pretty smelly, wearing the same coat everywhere he went. Winter or summer did not matter to him. He never changed that coat. Once he came over to our house with a turtle. They allowed Willard (my older brother) and myself to play with the turtle for approximately two or three hours. After I became bored with the animal, I left and went over to the next-door neighbor's house and began playing with them. Upon my return I noticed that the turtle was not to be found. I went to my brother Willard and asked him if he knew where the turtle was? He answered "yes"! Green coat had cut his head off, cracked his shell open and made turtle soup out of him. They even asked Willard and I if we would like some of the soup. Of course we both said "No thank you".

This is just one of the examples of things that Arthur Lee and his friends would do when they came over and hung out while drinking. They were very bad alcoholics, and they would often ask us to do silly things for them. Sometimes they would play a James Brown record and ask Willard and I to get on top of the coffee table and dance. I guess this was their way of having some form of entertainment. We kind of enjoyed it as well. You know as a child, any attention you received was good. Sometimes Arthur Lee treated my brothers and me very well, and other times it was as if we were toys or something. He owned a 1965 Ford Galaxy 500. This car was in very good shape. He seemed to care more about that car than he did about my mother. Everyday when he would come home, you could hear that car over a block away. He would burn rubber for approximately 1 block. This was just another showpiece or toy of his.

In 1971 my mother gathered all of us up along with our junk and we moved to the housing project at 463 Lenoir Court in River Rouge. Sometimes it seemed as if we moved every other week. This did not seem to be abnormal to us because we had become accustomed to moving all of the time. I never knew the feeling of stability and growing up in a home with a mother and father who worked and paid taxes. Our life was always in some sort of turmoil.

Arthur Lee had been sick for sometime now. We did not know what was wrong but I think that everybody could sense that it was not good. This was a man that I had never witnessed to be sick. I didn't think that anything in this world could bother him. I felt that he was indestructible. So when he became sick I knew it was not going to be a good outcome. On Easter Sunday mom gathered up the clan and we went to the Detroit Medical Center area to a hospital called Herman Kiefer. This is where indigent people were allowed to bring someone for treatment. We went there to see Arthur Lee. He was so sick that we were not allowed in the hospital to see him. We had to stand outside his hospital window and wave "hello" to him. At this point I thought to myself that I would probably never see him alive again. However two weeks later to everyone's surprise the hospital allowed him to come home. We were so happy to see him. I kept thinking to myself that everything was going to be all right now that daddy was home again. Somehow deep down on the inside of me though, I felt that something was still wrong. He could hardly walk and he was so frail that I almost did not recognize him.

Approximately seven days later we had to rush Arthur Lee back to the hospital again. All that I could remember was that horrible cough. It sounded as if he had pneumonia or something, a loud rattle after the initial cough. Sometime later we received a call from the doctor. It was bad news. Arthur Lee was DEAD! My mother became ill immediately. She fell directly to the floor as soon as I handed her the telephone and she went into cardiac arrest. So I quickly hung up the telephone and called 911. They told me to keep her comfortable and that the ambulance was on the way. My mom was in the hospital for a short period of time, maybe 4 days or so. One of my father's (Arthur Lee's) sisters came over and watched us while Momma was in the hospital. All I can remember about my step-aunt was that she was a nasty cook. Her food was terrible. She made a pineapple upside down cake for us that had wet dough in the middle when it was supposed to be done. I made sure that no one ate any of that cake.

When Arthur Lee died I felt a sense of emptiness. It was as if he was my real father. I remember once when I was sick, Arthur Lee picked me up and put me on his shoulders, carried me down 2 flights of stairs and put me in the back seat of his car. I still remember to this day how he burned rubber almost all the way down the street in an attempt to get me to the hospital as quickly as possible. In spite of all of his faults, I believed that he truly loved and cared for all of us, even though Willard and I were not his natural children. Whenever my brother and I would go anywhere with him, we would lean against the back seat of the car and sing, "Go daddy go" over and over again. Although he beat my mother all of the time, I never remember one incident of him hitting any of the children when he was drunk. We did receive punishment whenever the adults felt that it was appropriate.

Then there was the funeral! I remember thinking to myself that this is the first funeral that I have ever been to. I did not know what to expect. Of course now that my father was gone I felt that I had to take over the fatherly responsibilities. This is a God-given trait that I have always been blessed with. During the actual funeral one of my cousins said something that has burned into my memory for 30 years. His name was Bernard. He was approximately 7 years old, and there was some speculation that he could have been Arthur Lee's son as well. He walked up to the casket and peering over into it, turned looking puzzled and said, "Why is Arthur Lee lying in that box asleep?" At that instant I felt like jumping on him and beating some sense into him for his disrespect of the only father I had ever known. After the funeral we lost contact with Bernard and his mother.

When I was 10 years old, we all piled into a Greyhound bus and visited my grandparents in Georgia. My grandmother was very mean. She insisted that we say "Yes, Ma'am" and "Yes, Sir" whenever we addressed her or my grandfather. But that wasn't the mean part. It was the way she talked to my mother that I thought was a little rude. My mother was sitting on the porch with my grandparents while all of us children were chasing chickens and feeding the pigs. My grandmother would yell something at us and my mother would say it's "all right". My grandmother would then yell some directive at my mother as if she did not know how to raise us. That seemed a little mean to me. Especially since my mother had been away from

Georgia for about 10 years. You would think that my grandparents would have missed her. Well if my grandmother did she sure did not show it.

My grandfather on the other hand seemed to be a little whipped (wimpy) to me. I was only 10 years old. All of the examples of men that I had ever seen were strong and aggressive. So for me to see a passive man was a little stunning. My grandmother would yell in a loud voice "W.L., come here". My grandfather would literally drop whatever he was doing and run in the direction of my grandmother. During our visit I was blessed with the opportunity to meet quite a few of my relatives. However most of them were busy or working so I was not able to visit with them. I was allowed an opportunity to pick Crowder peas with my grandmother. All the time I was with her it was as if I was with a drill sergeant. She gave me orders every step of the way. I was very respectable to her however. Upon our return from picking peas, there was a "like new" Chevrolet in the driveway. It turned out that it was Booker T. whom I was led up this point to believe that he was my father. When I ran up to greet him I yelled "Daddy! Daddy! Daddy!" Then there was a five-second silence, and suddenly he, (Booker T.) turned and looked at me and said with disdain in his voice "YOU ARE NOT MY SON. GET AWAY FROM ME!" You can't know how this resounded in my very soul. To be told all of your life that this was your father, and for him to say something like that. After that small exchange my brother Willard ran up to him and said the same thing I did, only his reception was different. Willard was picked up by Booker T. and swung around in the air. He even gave him some money. My mother had always said to us before we traveled to Georgia that she never wanted to see Booker T. So when he arrived I did not find it unusual that she had gotten up and went in the house when she was previously sitting on the porch.

Needless to say I never asked my mom about this. I think it was because I knew what she was going through and I did not want to cause her any more sadness. So I never mentioned it.

LEARNING TO WORSHIP GOD!

Some of the things we go through in life seem to be simple but in actuality they are very complicated. While growing up in the small suburb of River Rouge, Michigan, I was given the opportunity to go to church with my friends, the Wardens. The Wardens would go to church every Sunday and on Wednesday they would go to Sunshine Band Practice. This is where I was first introduced to church lifestyle. Mind you at this time I did not know why I was going to church. I did not even understand the full meaning of church. All I knew was that when I was in pain there was someone that I could call on who would make me feel a whole lot better. And even though I could not see him physically, I've always felt that He was always right there whenever I needed him. When I talk to Jesus I have always received an answer. When Arthur Lee passed away, this was the very first time that I went to a church building. We never attended church while growing up on Holford Street.

This is not to say that my mother was not a woman of God. My mother is a wonderful woman. She prays daily and has a very wonderful and beautiful singing voice. When she was small her mother would make her and her sisters and brothers go to church every Sunday. Therefore, she did not want to force her children to go every Sunday. However she never discouraged us from going to church. As a matter of fact she would often say to me, "Boy, you need Jesus!" When I told her that I was going to church with the Wardens, she said that I should take my older brother Willard with me.

He (Willard) once told me that church was a scam. And that it was a way for preachers to get money from people by telling them they needed to come to church. I don't believe this was a lie, but I knew that everyone has problems sometimes even preachers. So every time I would mention that I was going to church, my brother would call me a punk. I remember one time when he wanted me to lie for him. I told him that I was not interested in lying for him or anyone else. He became very agitated with me and dumped a full can of beer on me. He did this while there were some of his friends standing with him. So you see it wasn't always easy for me to worship God when I was young.

Quite often I was ridiculed for being "soft". Most of my friends would say that I was weak or not as strong as the other young men in my immediate circle of friends were. But I never let that talk discourage me. I knew that somewhere down the line, my way of thinking would pay off for me. Now my brother Willard is suffering from lung cancer and will have to go through lung surgery very soon. I'm glad that I haven't compromised my way of thinking to please man. Although I have not always lived the way I should, I know that my God sits on high, and He sees the things that we have done in life to please Him. And even my brother, who persecuted me for going to church when I was young, now has allowed me to pray for his healing. The thing that is pretty amazing about this whole story is that I truly believe that GOD can heal him if that is my heart's desire and God's will for his life. HALLELUJAH!

During these years of my life I would often listen very intently to older people and adults, as they would fill my life with wisdom. I have always been able to talk to adults more easily than I could talk to young people of my own age group. I wish I could tell you that there was some adult who influenced me to go the way I have chosen to go, but there wasn't. Probably the only adult who had an influence in my life was and still is my mother.

My mother would always tell me if something was right or wrong, and how I should go about doing things, when I felt that the decision was difficult. She was not a typical mother in that there was no man to instruct her in the proper way to raise a young man. I guess that is why I respect her so much. Because even though she was not blessed with all of the resources in life, she still did a pretty good job with all of us.

Mrs. Warden was blessed to have a husband and parents in close proximity to her while she raised her family. The Wardens seemed never to want for anything. They always had new clothes and toys. Whenever they wanted an item it would only be a short waiting period before they would receive whatever gift they had a desire for. This was not the case however in our family. We would never get the items we asked for. I don't feel that this was a disadvantage to us however. We learned at an early age, that if you wanted something you had to go out and earn the money to buy it yourself. I think that this is what kept us out of jail. My brother Willard and I worked on the milk truck to earn extra money whenever there was something we wanted to buy.

During those precious years of my life I would often get into fights in the old neighborhood for being different. At the time I did not realize that fighting would not solve my problems. I thought that in order to be respected you had to fight. Even though I attended church with the Wardens I would not allow people to talk bad about me. I would not allow people to talk bad about any of my siblings without taking my fist to their mouth. I guess this too was a good lesson for me because as I grew up and got older I began to realize that because of my young fighting escapades the kids did not bother me.

I remember a time before we moved away from Holford Street, when I would be leaving Northrop School each day. I must have been in the second or third grade. After school ended on my way out of the front door a very large bully would wait for me to leave the school so that he could beat me up everyday. I was held and punched by this bully everyday for the whole school year. Once I ran home crying and I told my stepfather (ARTHUR LEE), that a bully was beating me up everyday after school. He told me that if I ever came in the house crying again because someone beat me up, I would receive another whipping from him. So needless to say I never came home crying again. Mind you the bully did not stop beating me up. I just started fighting back.

This is probably where I received that fighting back mentality that has stuck with me all of my life. Growing up in the projects gave me plenty of opportunities to fight. There were two different types of individuals growing up in my neighborhood, the 'have's' and the 'have-nots.' If you lived in the projects you were automatically grouped in with the have-nots. However if you lived in a regular home with a mortgage and two parents you were considered as part of the have group. My friends the Wardens lived in the projects with us but somehow the children in my peer group put them in the "I have group". I think it was because they could get just about anything that they wanted to get even though they lived in the projects.

So being in the "have-nots" group made it difficult for me to fit in with the regular group, and whenever I tried it I ended up in a fight. Most of the fights were pretty meaningless. However there were a few epic battles worth remembering. There was once a fight between a gang called the Schaefer Players and the back street. Everyone who lived on the back street was involved in the fight. The Schaefer Players did not fight fair however. They had guns, knives and weapons. And we went to a gunfight with nail clippers. One thing was for certain though. They knew they had been in a fight when it was all over. People were bleeding and crying. We were lucky that no one was seriously injured.

Another one of our battles happened at the high school. It was between the whites and the blacks.

The white people did not like us and we did not care for them either. So of course the only way to settle a dispute was to pick up a chair and throw it across the room. The whites literally lived across the railroad tracks. That's right. You hear on television about people living across the tracks all the time. However we actually did live across the tracks from the white people who went to school with us.

It wasn't until I began attending River Rouge High School that I realized that white people lived in our city. We were so separated that the young black people in the neighborhood did not even know that white people were a part of our city. As we grew older, we attempted to understand why riots would constantly breakout in our city. We began to realize that most of our problems stemmed from being so separated in everything that we did.

So you see even though I was a young Christian, I still had some things that God was trying to clean out of me. I was learning through trial and error what to do and what not to do in life. Praise God! I'm so glad that He protected me as I went through my early years of not knowing how to live and get along with people. And I thank God that he has brought me this far.

MY CROSS TO BEAR!

During the young years of my life, I can only remember small amounts of time. This is because I was born with a disease called Sickle Cell Anemia. Most Caucasian people refer to this as the "BLACK MAN'S" disease. I've learned however that this is not true. There are Indians and a small amount of white's who have this disease as well.

Sickle Cell Anemia is a blood disorder that is passed down from family members. It is a hereditary condition that is caused by each parent having the sickle cell trait and passing it on to his or her offspring. If both parents have the Sickle Cell trait a certain percentage (4%) of their children will be at risk of being born with the full-blown Sickle Cell disease and not just the trait of the disease. If one parent has the disease then the children born to this relationship will be at a greater risk of being born with the disease. My father was not alive when I got older and attempted to locate him to find out if he had the disease or not. So therefore I never knew if both of my parents had the disease or not.

This disease caused me to be sick every week. I was in the hospital one week and home one week. The only thing they knew about the disease in 1966 was that it caused severe pain. Whenever I went to the hospital they would always look at me as if I was strange or something. It's as if they thought I was faking or something. I had the feeling that if my arm wasn't broken or my leg hanging off, they couldn't tell if any thing was wrong with me.

The truth of the matter is that Sickle Cell disease is a condition that causes your blood cells to be shaped differently. The average person's blood cells are shaped like round circles, but my blood cells, and anyone, who has Sickle Cell Anemia, has cells that are shaped like half moons. This causes the cells to bunch up in all of the bends and curves of the body, like the elbows or the back of the legs behind the knees. When they bunch up it causes severe pain because the blood cannot travel to the vital areas of the body to function the way the blood system was designed by God to perform.

When your blood is trapped in the bends of your body it causes a circulatory system problem, and it also prevents the blood system from carrying the essential vitamins and minerals through the body so that they can feed your internal organs the way they should. This is why doctors would say that people with this disease would not live a long life.

Every time I went to the hospital I would get a new doctor, and he would have to do a brand new study on why I was hurting. Meanwhile I'm lying on the table in excruciating pain. For a four-year-old child this was pretty traumatic. If you ask me, I think it was borderline abuse.

I did not understand it at the time but later on I discovered that the medication I was receiving was a narcotic. The only treatment I could receive from the hospital was pain medication and liquid (IV) intravenous. The narcotic would stop the pain while the IV would cause the blood to circulate better. It's like receiving a bandage for a stab wound. I believe that receiving this narcotic while I was a young child contributed to my eventually becoming addicted to drugs. Now I do not think that I could have survived without the drugs, but I do believe that more research should have been done on the disease and possible treatments for the disease, which in turn would have given me a better opportunity to succeed in life.

However like I've said over and over again I would not change anything in my life that I have gone through. Everything I've experienced was for a purpose. God had a plan for me so I had to go through everything that I have gone through in order for me to fulfill my purpose in life. Unwittingly the doctors that examined me when I was small were all a part of a greater plan in life.

Once when I was young I was given a shot of penicillin. I had a high fever from what was discovered to be pneumonia. Penicillin is a commonly used anti-biotic to which I was highly allergic. I went into a coma for 72 hours. I thought I was going to die. As a matter of fact I was clinically dead for a short period of time. Contrary to popular belief, I did not have a life-changing experience while lying on the hospital bed in a coma. But I do remember floating above the bed and watching everyone that entered the room including my mother who would sit and cry most of the days that she would visit me.

Needless to say when you go through so much as a young person, it makes you grow up real quick. Although I had problems as a young black man trying to grow up in America, I still felt that I was here for a purpose. During this bout of unconsciousness, I felt that I was fully aware of everything that was going on. I just couldn't move a muscle. I remember when they came in my room and put ice cubes all around my body. There was a plastic bag draped around my bed and I was lying very still. Being in a coma is a very scary position to be in. Your body is limp and your vital signs, like your heartbeat, pulse, and respiration are very slow and barely detectable. If the attending doctor does not know what he is doing you could be diagnosed as (DOA) Dead on Arrival. So you see being in a coma is a very serious state of being.

After I came out of this coma I would still feel that something was missing from my life. Everyday I would wake up and think to myself, "Why am I here? What is my purpose?" I knew that there had to be a reason for my existence. I could not understand why God would create a young man who was sick all of the time and could not accomplish anything he tried to do. As I grew older, I began to understand that every person in the earth has a purpose, including me, and that God created me. This is true. But the consequences of this existence is not God's doing. God has allowed sin in the world so that he can reveal His power to the world. The Bible says "Many are the afflictions of the righteous: but the LORD delivereth him out of them all." (PSALMS 34:19) So you see I was born with a disease, this is true. This disease however is a direct result of the sin of Adam. But you see I've been delivered from that sin with the blood bought sacrifice of our Lord and Savior Jesus Christ. I can choose to live for this disease or I can choose to live for God. Because God is the only one who is able to heal me of this disease. I choose to live for God! You see the world has already given me their testimony about this disease. The world says that we don't know anything about this disease, and that all we can do is treat the symptoms of it. But "Jesus said unto him, if thou canst believe, all things are possible to him that believeth." (St. Mark 9:23) I choose to believe GOD'S report.

So you see even though I have this affliction it has not stopped God's purpose for my life. I believe that through this affliction God is going to get some glory out of my life. I'm already convinced that He is my deliverer and protector and also my healer. I have seen so much in my life that this has to be a blessing to someone who is suffering from some sort of disability. So if you are going through something in your life and you think you just can't make it through, just know that somewhere there is someone who just might be going through more than you are.

PAIN!

Hurting physically is only part of the pain a person feels when they have a crisis. I think that the mental pain is more painful than the physical. However the physical is quite astonishing and unbelievable. Most people would not want to deal with this type of pain. I remember a passage in the Bible where Job cursed the day he was born because of his pain.

"And Job spoke and said, let the day perish where in I was born, and the night in which it was said, there is a man-child conceived." (Job 3:3-10) I've known people in my lifetime that did not deal with pain in their lives. They decided to get drunk or to get high, to drown out the pain. I've even known a few people who decided to end it rather than deal with the pain.

I once knew a young man named Anthony who had asthma. We went to school together and hung around the old neighborhood together. He loved to play basketball. One day he was playing basketball on an outdoor court in the old neighborhood. He went home and laid down and died when he could not catch his breath. You see when you have asthma you loose your breath and need a breathing treatment after exercising for an extended period of time.

There were many times that he and I both were sick after playing sports. When I went home and rocked back and forth with pain, I always called on God for help. But this day I believe that Anthony went home and said, "I give up." I believe that he probably refused his breathing treatment and became frustrated with getting sick all of the time, as he would occasionally do from time to time while in my presence.

The physical attributes of pain are what most people think of whenever a person mentions the word "pain". But psychologically when a person is in pain for a long stretch of time, he begins to automatically rationalize the pain. How can I make this pain less intense, or how can I discover a more comfortable way to deal with this pain? So the mind tends to work on a very high level while suffering through physical pain.

But there is good news! All pain is not bad pain. Some pain is important and some pain is essential for our overall growth. If it had not been for the pain that Dr. Martin Luther King Jr. suffered, we would not have the right to participate in the Democratic process.

That's right. Voting is a right. Someone suffered pain in order that you may have the right to express your opinion through the ballot box and make a difference in the way this country is governed. People suffered pain in the 1940's to establish unions, so companies could not just fire you when they felt like it.

And last but definitely not least of all, Jesus Christ suffered pain when He was crucified for the sins of the world. I thank and praise God now for the pain, because it's in the pain that we overcome all the effects of the world. It's in the pain that we become closer to the Father. I thank GOD for the pain. In the pain I have learned to grow stronger, and I've learned that trouble won't last always and that pain builds character.

Playing sports was a dream of mine but each time I would try to play, it would make me sick. Therefore I would rarely get picked. This was in elementary through high school. Whenever I was picked, I would play for an extended amount of time, and my body would ache all over.

When the other children would see me in so much pain, they would have puzzled looks on their faces. This caused me to be treated funny by my classmates. They did not understand what Sickle Cell Anemia was all about. Neither did I understand the true meaning of this disease. So trying to explain what is wrong with you when you don't completely understand the thing that you are trying to explain, is not only difficult, but it is almost impossible.

Most of the young people I grew up with had never heard of the disease before. They thought I had something that could be caught, like a cold or something. Therefore no one wanted to be around me. During the young days of my life it was important to be accepted by my friends and family members. My older brother had already showed me that he did not respect me, so it was important to me to gain the acceptance of my friends. So I would never talk about my disease. Most of my peers did not even know that I had Sickle Cell. It was very hard to keep it a secret for so long, but somehow I pulled it off. My friends that were very close to me were the only ones who knew.

My friend's mother Mrs. Warden once told me that I would die before I reached the age of twenty-one. So I took this information to my doctor and asked him if this was true. Dr. Amanula of the Wayne County General Hospital told me that in most cases this was true. My heart sunk when he told me that. Then I started to pray! I asked my Daddy if this was true. Daddy said, "Not so"! HALLELUJAH!

Not until after I graduated from high school did my friends find out about my condition. To understand the type of pain I was in, you'd have to ask a woman who has the disease. I was once a member of the Sickle Cell Center, where I met a woman who had the disease. She said that giving birth did not even compare to the pain you have from a crisis. So now you get some idea of how much it hurts.

Being a man it is almost impossible to get an understanding of childbirth. Since I have been called to the ministry however, now I have a new revelation on birth, and being pregnant, and all of the things that lead up to giving birth to that which has been deposited into the innermost parts of your sanctuary. When God deposits the very seeds of life into your belly, you ache all over until you are allowed to go into labor and push the very essence of your existence out of your mouth. I'm not a doctor but I believe that if a woman was pregnant and she refused to push after the nine months of incubation and growth, that she would not only kill the life inside of her, but that she would probably lose her own life as well.

You see giving birth does not only benefit the person who is pregnant, but it also benefits the person who is witnessing this birth. When a person gives birth to a seed that seed is planted and it grows roots and those roots develop into a tree, and that tree provides fruit, and that fruit begins the very essence of life for the person who is fed by that fruit.

Pain is quite amazing in that it causes a person to think very intensely about what is important in life. Most people suffer some form of pain. To some it's emotional and to others it's spiritual and still others it's physical. But it's all pain. The thing to remember is that pain and suffering won't last always.

A SECOND CHANCE AT FATHERHOOD

When I was 11 years old, my mother met a man named Ervin. She became involved with this guy. He was a sinner who did not want to hear anything about God. He was a heavy drinker, who was very short in stature. This caused him to exhibit a Napoleon complex. He seemed to feel the need to give orders to everyone. Ervin worked for an asphalt paving company, which caused him to smell very bad with the smell of asphalt and fuel oil all over his body. He seemed not to like to take baths very regularly as well. Frankly I do not see what my mother found interesting in a man like this anyway. But she developed a relationship with him and eventually she gave birth to my two youngest siblings Regina and Angelic during this relationship.

Needless to say, I did not get along with him. As a young child I could not understand how a person could drink alcohol and think that it was okay. The law does not say that it is illegal, so the world thinks that it is all right to drink until you can't stand up straight.

But I don't feel the same. I believe that drinking is just as bad as using illegal drugs. Any mind-altering drug used to subdue some conscience feeling or thought should be outlawed. However my Father has taught me to hate the sin and not the sinner. I believe that this chapter of my life had also contributed in some small way to my overall addiction to drugs and cigarettes. Ervin was a very heavy smoker. He probably smoked two to three packs of cigarettes a day. I remember watching him drag on a cigarette. He made it look so good. He was one of those people who inhaled very deeply but he never blew out the smoke. He would begin to talk and the smoke would escape from his nose and mouth as he talked.

I found it quite ironic that he would let a pack of cigarettes burn up in the ashtray because he was usually too drunk to finish smoking his cigarette once he lit it. His routine was to come home from work and go into the back bedroom, arguing to himself the whole time, and change his clothes. Mind you we never heard any water run when he did this. Then he would walk around the corner from the bedroom and go into the kitchen. The next sound you would hear was a beer can opening and him sliding half of it down his throat in one gulp. Then he sat down at the dinner table and began going through his mail. After opening his mail and smoking about ten cigarettes he would turn to my mother and say something stupid like, "Are you coming to bed tonight?" My mother would begin to curse him like a sailor for being drunk.

Ervin had a bad habit of coming home and starting an argument with my mother, which usually lead to a physical confrontation between them. So not only was he an alcoholic, but he was also a woman beater. Several times, as a young man, who did not know his purpose, I wanted to really put a hurting on him for hitting my mother. I know lots of people who would have done just that. However the God in me would not allow me to do it. Here is an example. Once when I was sick, and lying in the back seat of our 1972 Cadillac, I overheard him say to my mother, "I WISH THAT NIGGER WOULD LIE DOWN AND DIE". As a little child you don't quite know how to take something like that. I can't imagine someone having that much hatred in his heart for an individual. I believe that even then my light was beginning to shine. Because if it had not been for God, in this instance, when I recovered I would have confronted him about what he said while taking me to the hospital.

Growing up in the ghetto as a young African American male is tough enough. Without a father it's even tougher. Ervin turned out to be the only "father figure" I ever knew. The reason I say this is because he was the only father that was constantly around; the only one I could grab the lessons of life from. You see in order for a youth to become a man, he needs an example or a father figure; a person who can deposit life into the history of his mind so that as he goes through life he is able to draw from his memories in his life. The lessons I learned from him however did not help me in life. They actually caused more pain than good. He would often say that you have to get a job so that you could have the things in life that you want. But then he never got anything in life that he wanted even though he worked for approximately 30 years of his life.

What is ironic about this situation is that my mother, the one he beat all the time, ended up being the one who cleaned his butt when he was too ill to do it himself. You see he eventually came down with cancer. It caused him to be completely bedridden. Ervin passed away shortly after contracting cancer. What was pretty amazing about his story was that he accepted Jesus Christ, as his personal Savior, while on his deathbed. My wife Terri would go over to his house with my mother to help take care of him while he was ill. During her visits with him she would minister to him concerning Jesus Christ, and the gift of God. Not only did he accept Jesus, but I did his eulogy and preached his funeral as well. Doing the eulogy was not difficult for me at all. It was probably because I saw him suffer so much during his illness and during the later stages of his disability. I was in the process of studying for the ministry. Pastor Robert Cuffie of Praise Christian Tabernacle was training me.

Ervin lost all of his weight and was almost unrecognizable during the last days of his life. He was also the father of four other children from a previous relationship. He was divorced with four kids when he met my mother. All of his children were grown and out of the house. We did not see them much. But at the funeral they all showed up to see what they could get. To their surprise however there was nothing to get. Ervin died penniless with an outstanding mortgage, two raggedy cars and nothing else. I am thankful however because at the funeral, God touched his children. One of his daughters approached me after the funeral and inquired about joining my church.

I praise God for that because when I accepted my calling to the ministry, I was a little bit skeptical. I had not received confirmation that this was the direction the Lord wanted me to go. But during a sermon I preached at Praise Christian Tabernacle, a young lady started crying and walked up to the altar and asked what she must do to be saved. As if that was not enough when Sherri Sutherland started crying and asked the same question after her father's funeral, I felt that was confirmation enough that what I was doing was what God called me to do.

In this chapter of my life, I received a great deal of instruction. As you can see alcohol was a major part of my life up until this point. Every man that has been involved in my life has either been an alcoholic or on their way to becoming one. So when you see a young African American male, don't be so quick to judge him. Alcohol has probably been the single common thread in his life. I believe that the men in my life did not realize how bad they were damaging my future by their actions. Thank God that I was chosen before the foundation of the world to be a disciple of Christ, and that He has not allowed me to be influenced by the lessons of my life.

THE FOUNDATION OF MY LIFE
THROUGH CHRIST

The very first job I ever worked was when I was seven years old. I worked for a man named Walt S. on the Twin Pines Milk truck. He drove the truck through the neighborhood delivering milk to people and I would help by taking milk to the neighbors that he did not go to. I was paid fifty cents a day and half of a gallon of milk or ice cream. When I was fourteen I got a real job working at Kentucky Fried Chicken. This job only lasted one day. The guy I was working with decided to walk off the job, and he convinced me to do so as well. This was a very important lesson for me, because I was fired, but the guy who convinced me to walk off, kept his job and laughed at me as well.

My next job was a summer job in the summer program at River Rouge High School. We used to call them Cognac's; named after the man who ran the program. When I got my first check from my Coogan I think I was the happiest man in the world. Not just because I had money, but because my mother did not have any, and this was my opportunity to show her that I was her little man. So I cashed my first check and went to the grocery store, because we did not have any food in the refrigerator. Just to see the look on my mother's face was reward enough for me.

My life has hit some bumps in the road this is true. Another bump in the road was when my son was born. He was born on November 1, 1983. I gave him my name, because at the time his mother and I were planning to get married but things did not work out for us. However I thank and praise God for the experience. Remember I said earlier that I would not change one aspect of my life. Roger Jr. is my Ishmael and I love every fiber of his tall, skinny body. You see it wasn't time for the promise that God had for my life yet, but I wanted to go out and make it happen before it was time. It was just another bump.

I can't say that it was YOLLESHA'S fault that things did not turn out right, and I can't say that it was my fault either. But whatever the reason, I believe that I am with the person that God intended me to be with.

Once while growing up in Ecorse, Michigan and attending high school there, my mother became a partner with her sister, my Aunt Trudy Eady, in a restaurant on Visger Road in Ecorse, Michigan.

During this chapter in my life I learned a lot about people, and how the ones that you think are your friends can quickly change and become your enemies. I was usually in charge of going to the warehouse and picking up supplies for my aunt.

During this chapter Yollesha was my girlfriend. Maybe I should give you some history of our relationship together. When we first met I broke my kneecap and was laid up in bed for a while. During this time Yollesha left me and began seeing a guy named Degbert. She started sleeping with this guy, and soon became pregnant. After she became pregnant Degbert decided to leave her.

By then my leg had healed and I was back out on the street doing my thing once again. I happened to run into Yollesha and she was as pregnant as can be. Everyone said to me that I should leave her alone, because she was no good. "If she could leave you because you broke your leg then she would never be able to stay faithful to you." But how many people know that as a child whenever someone says to you that you can't have something that's the very thing you go for just because they said you can't have it.

That's the way I felt about Yollesha. Everyone including my Aunt Trudy told me to leave her alone, but I said to my aunt that she did not know what she was talking about. This caused us to have a serious disagreement. It almost turned into a knock down drag out fistfight. My aunt said things to me that until this time I had never heard from an adult outside of my household before. She said that I was dying of blood cancer.

That's the first time I had ever heard someone refer to my Sickle Cell Anemia as blood cancer before. She was angry because I told her that she was an alcoholic. This was true and still is true to this day. Anyway to bring this story to an end, my aunt wanted me to know that Yollesha was no good for me and I did not want to listen.

Shortly after this incident I was back in a relationship with Yollesha. Shortly after that, we got an apartment in River Rouge and my son was born. When I got this apartment in River Rouge I asked Ervin, my mother's boyfriend, to co-sign a loan for me to get a car. He told me he would, so I went to the credit union and began the paperwork to get the loan. I applied for the loan to get a car so that I could make it to work. I was a security guard working at Metropolitan Airport at the time. However I was finding it more and more difficult to get to work everyday. Sometimes Yollesha's mother would take me and sometimes I would get a ride with a friend or my mother. All of this was getting old very quickly. I wanted to be able to do for myself without asking anyone for help.

After I finished the paperwork for the credit union, I asked Ervin to come with me so that he could sign his part. So he drove down to the credit union with me and took one look at the paperwork for the $800 loan, and said "No". This "no" was resounding. I could not believe that he would make me go through filling out all of this paperwork to say "No". On the ride back home I noticed that he had a beer in his lap and that he was pretty toasted already. However I was not that upset. I guess I kind of expected something like that from him. He had never done anything like this for me before. Eventually the credit union granted me the loan without a co-signer. I can remember praying and asking my Father for help. He finally answered me.

Later on that year Ervin was asked the same question by one of my younger brothers. Not only did he say "Yes", he actually did it for him. Talk about hatred. I think that would be a good definition of it right here. I don't believe that this was Ervin's fault. The enemy knew that I was starting to understand my calling, and he was trying to throw a monkey wrench in God's plan.

ENTANGLED IN THE AFFAIRS OF THIS WORLD

As I grew older in life, many problems seemed to attach themselves to me. Up until this point in my life I'd only to concern myself with alcohol abuse by other people. But now I start to use drugs myself. So you see the longer you are around abusive situations, the more likely it is to become a part of your life eventually.

During high school I found myself attempting to be a part of the in-crowd. I experimented with marijuana use and became addicted to the drug. Because of my illness I was unable to drink alcohol. Most of my high school friends were beginner alcoholics. Therefore when my so-called friends would drink to have what they considered to be, "a good time", I would roll a joint. This led to me being known for having weed all the time. Pretty soon I was known as the "weed man". I would skip school, buy some weed, roll a bag full of joints and sell them. My mother was not aware that I had chosen this path in life. I think she probably had an idea but she never said anything to me about my marijuana usage.

Once while she and I were sitting around talking, as we would occasionally do, she told me that she knew I was using weed. She said that she thought it was therapeutic for me with my Sickle Cell. In a way she was right. Whenever I smoked it, I did notice the pain would stop.

During a visit to the hospital I confided in a doctor about my smoking weed. He said that I was not the first young man with Sickle Cell that said marijuana seemed to stop the pain during a crisis. He was careful to tell me that he was not endorsing my drug abuse, but he said he would not tell me to stop either if it was working. So you see that then I had some legal justification for what I was doing.

I think this is probably one of the reasons why I did it for so long, because I did not see anything wrong with what I was doing. Not only was this my justification, but my mother was not complaining about the money she would receive from me, from time to time. This was justification as well. I had discovered a new way to get money. From this point on I was never without income again. Most of my life I grew up on welfare. Food stamps would only go so far.

You have to understand that for a young man who has never had anything to suddenly have money, and not have to want for anything, it is a pretty good feeling.

All of a sudden I became a very popular person at school. The girls liked me, and the guys wanted to be my friend. All my life I grew up with not so many friends because of my illness, but then I started to find friends everywhere I went. And these friends did not care if I was sickly or not.

My head was in such a cloud, literally and physically that I thought what I was doing wasn't wrong. Soon the weed wasn't enough. I needed something more. This is when I discovered cocaine; soon after that, crack.

This is a drug directly from hell. One puff from a crack cigarette and I was addicted. It would take me seven years to shake this habit. My addiction to cocaine happened very suddenly.

I started a new job at K-mart. This is where I met a young man named Linck. Linck introduced me to powder cocaine. He even showed me how to snort it. We would go into the restroom and have a snort while at work. Soon my marijuana customers were asking me for coke.

Linck would have a large packet of coke envelopes with a rubber band around them. He would sell me a packet of powder in a small Glad bag, and I would have to separate the powder, add some cut to it and put it in an envelope. Each envelope would contain twenty-five dollars worth of powder cocaine. It would sell like hot cakes. You would not believe the people who were addicted to cocaine. I had lawyers and nurses as customers. High-leveled businessmen would come and look for me.

This drug used to frighten me. I would think to myself "Anything this strong has to be illegal and deadly." But that did not stop me from wanting to deal it more and more. Eventually I became addicted to cocaine and I needed more of it for myself. As time went on things began to get a little tight at K-mart so I had to find another job. I noticed myself becoming more paranoid about everything. I think this was the drug causing me to feel this way. But I decided to get another job anyway.

I began working at a screw machine shop in Livonia. I had to stop using for a little while to retain this job. Thank God! I signed up for rehabilitation at Sumby Hospital on Visger Road in River Rouge, Michigan. This was my first stay in a rehabilitation hospital. However I knew it was necessary if I was to get my life back in order. It was never my intent to get addicted to the drugs that I was selling to make a living. However crack does not care what your purpose for using it is. After witnessing the abuse in my family because of drinking and addiction I did not want the same thing to happen to me. While I was admitted in this hospital I met a couple of gentlemen who taught me some valuable lessons in dealing drugs. So you see my rehabilitation stay was more educational than anything else was.

Thanks be unto the Lord who gives me the victory. If it had not been for the Lord, I would still be addicted. My God is able to make all grace abound toward me.

After a short stint in the Army, and a semester of community college, I was introduced to the love of my life, Mrs. Terri A. (Starr) Moore. She means more to me than I mean to myself. From the very first day that I met her I knew she was going to be my wife.

When I met her she was in a relationship with a young man who was in the Air Force. The last time he came home he caused her a lot of pain. I told her that it was time for her to have a real man, a man who was willing to stay right here with her and help her to make it. Someone who would not just come around and constantly take. When I met my wife her father was suffering from cancer. This is when I discovered what having a real father was all about. Willie Byron Starr, Sr. affectionately known as "Pete" taught me a lot. I discovered what it meant to be a real man and a responsible father. To see his mortality in this way was a very valuable lesson to me. Although I have never said anything to my wife about it, her father taught me how to be a real man. When I looked at him I did not just see a man that was dying but I saw a father who was loved by his family, a man who chose to stay with his wife and love his family through the good and the bad. Mr. Starr was married to his wife Ethel Sue (Green) Starr for 30 plus years. If that is not a good example of how to be a real man, then I just don't have a clear understanding of what is.

When I first saw my wife she was with her nephew Bruce. He was about six or seven years old at the time. I told her that I thought he was her son. She told me that he was her sister's boy. Bruce favors my wife a great deal. However when I met her older sister Deborah, then I understood why Bruce looks so much like my wife. In most families there is always someone who looks alike. And in this family Deborah and Terri could pass for twins if it wasn't for the age discrepancy.

My wife happens to be the youngest of six children. She has two older brothers. Raymond is the oldest and Brian is next in line. She has three sisters, Deborah, the oldest, Sherri and Valerie. At first it appeared that I was going to be able to get along with her siblings very well. I noticed that all of them were very nice. Her sisters were especially fun to be around. Valerie and Sherri could be, and probably should be comedians. Deborah is the more serious of the three older siblings.

Deborah strikes me as a more stable individual, someone who has her head on straight. That is she knows what she wants and she won't stop until she gets it. She works for the U.S. Post Office, where she has been employed since she graduated from high school. She was one of the lucky, or should I say blessed ones, who got a job right out of high school. I tried to find a job right out of high school, but all they told me was "sorry we're not accepting applications at this time". When I look at my wife's older sister, I see a picture of responsibility. She has two kids that she is raising on her own. She has a good paying job and she's not even asking for help from the father of the children. This is something I have never seen before. Every woman I have ever known has always attempted to make the father of the children they had together, regret the day he ever laid eyes on her, by registering with the Friend of the Court, or by prosecuting him. I'm not saying this is right or wrong. I'm only expressing to you that it has been my experience to only come across this type of woman.

I believe that men and women should follow God's plan for pro-creation, and wait until they are married to have sex. However I realize that not all people understand God and His plan for their lives, and that most young people use the wrong part of their anatomy to do their thinking for them. Having said that, I believe that Deborah, just like most of us, has made some bad decisions in her life. However she is not sitting around feeling sorry for herself or helpless. She's gotten up and done something about it. So I take my hat off to her for her courage and for her persistence.

She has two children, Bruce and Christopher. Bruce was around two and Christopher was not born yet when I first met my wife. As time went on, I noticed that these two young boys had the finest of clothes. They were wearing gym shoes that I could not afford to buy and wear for myself. When I saw that, I thought she was rich or real close to being rich. I had never seen little children dress this way before.

As I got to know my wife and her family, I began to realize that we were probably as different as night is from the day. She had a mother and a father, they owned a home and both of them had a job. Terri's father worked for Standard Tube Steel Company for almost thirty years before he retired from there. Shortly after retiring he discovered he had cancer. When I met my wife her father was suffering from cancer.

I could tell when I first met her father that he was ill and not doing very well. He appeared to be quite fragile and weak. However, his illness did not take away from his stern fatherly ways. I admired him for his ability to remain the head of his household even in his condition.

I thank God for my experience with Mr. Starr. He gave me a true understanding of what it meant to be a man. He was strong yet gentle, kind yet firm. Once when he asked me to change the oil in his 1978 Cadillac DeVille, I agreed. When I began changing the oil I became stuck when the oil filter would not come loose. Mr. Starr saw me struggling and yelled at me in a very firm and sincere voice. "I thought you knew how to change oil!" My first reaction was to get angry, but before I could say anything, Mr. Starr apologized for yelling at me. I had never seen that before. Grown men never apologized for their actions, or at least this was my experience up to this point.

I saw a lot of myself in Mr. Starr. He had a slight streak of mean in him, just like me. He was small in stature and ill with cancer. I've been ill all of my life and Deborah was always teasing me about how skinny my legs are. So you see when I look at him I see me. Friends and family always told me that a girl looks for someone who reminds her of her father for a husband. If this is true then Mr. Starr and I are more alike than I realize.

Not long after getting to know Mr. Starr he became seriously ill. His arm began to swell up and become immobile. Once, while assisting him up from a chair on the porch I accidentally grabbed his arm. This gave me a real understanding of how painful this cancer must be.

During this period of time in my relationship with my wife, I realized that in order for me to continue our relationship, I would need to get a job. So I asked my wife to help me with my resume. She helped me to find a job at a place called Life Unlimited. This was a workshop for mentally challenged adults. This job did not pay very well, but it was a good experience for me to work there. While I was employed at Life Unlimited I met another young lady. This is not a part of my life that I am very proud of, however I feel that it is very important.

Her name was Chantal. She was quite tall, and she stood about six feet two inches tall. Whenever my wife mentions her she calls her an "Amazon". She has a light complexion and long hair. My wife has always said to me that guys only went after girls that were light skinned with long hair. She seems to think that this is the reason why she could not find a decent man.

Chantal was very nice and a little lonely I think. We seemed to gravitate toward each other. When I came out of rehabilitation girls started to notice me. I was lost in the clouds for so many years. I guess I felt like I had to make up for some lost time. So I did not feel guilty about becoming involved with Chantal. That's right. Even though I was engaged to my wife I still became involved with this young lady. I told her about Terri and Terri about her. Well as you probably have already guessed they did not like each other.

In this chapter of my life it seemed as if I was looking for love in all the wrong places. I know this now. However you could not have convinced me that I was doing something wrong then. Deep down on the inside I knew it was wrong, but at this point in my life I was searching for my identity. I knew I was worth more than what I had been told all of my life.

This relationship lasted about six months. I always felt that Chantal had another guy on the side. During the time I wasted with her I found out there was another guy she was seeing. He was a professional basketball player who was playing overseas. I remember one incident when my wife had a confrontation with Chantal and me. I did not have a car so every once in a while I would get a ride home by Chantal. At this time I was living with my mother in the projects.

While sitting outside my mother's house talking, Terri drove up in her father's car. She began yelling and screaming at me to come here and leave that slut alone. So I got out of the car with Chantal and got in the car with Terri. I calmed her down and told her that I would call her as soon as Chantal left. Well as you probably have guessed she was not satisfied with that for an answer, so I told her to go home and leave me alone. Something my wife refused to do. So after an extensive and exhaustive conversation with Chantal and Terri I decided to break it off with Chantal and continue my relationship with my wife.

My wife showed me during this episode in my life that she was truly on my side. I have never had a person to be that dedicated to me. It appears that she truly does love me, and that what she has to say is not just a lot of meaningless rhetoric. Most of the women I have met in my life have always been quick to say, "I love you", but a very small number of them actually meant what they said.

I don't know if it was because of the abuse I faced growing up or just because I was lonely, but to see my wife stand by me even as I was being the biggest "idiot" in the world, really did something to me. It made me feel as if someone actually cared about me. This was a new feeling for me. I mean my mother cared about me but it was pretty generic. She cared about all of her kids. In general we all have someone in life that cares about us. But when you find that person who shows a genuine love and concern for what happens to you, it becomes a real life changing moment.

Right after this incident I decided to be completely faithful to my wife. I did not do it for show. I did it because I actually loved her. I loved her for how she loved me!

My wife had a friend named Torri, who lived right down the street from her. They grew up attending school together. When I met my wife

Torri's mother was already in heaven. She was left with the family house. She was an only child with a child of her own. Apparently she too had made some mistakes in life. Anyway because of my past and the type of person that I appear to portray to people who don't know me, I have become the kind of guy that my wife's family does not like. Her family's advice to her was to find another guy or go back to Chuck. This didn't settle well with my wife. She was just as determined, as I was to make our relationship work. So my wife moved in with Torri, her best friend.

Of course this did not settle well with my wife's family. They seemed to develop a real hatred for me and for Torri. I thought that it would be a temporary problem, but it turned out to last a whole lot longer than I thought it would. It turns out they were upset with me all the way up until the wedding, and beyond.

During the early days of our relationship, before we were married, I would attend church with my wife. Eventually I joined her church. At the time she was attending St. James Missionary Baptist Church. I believe this is where my wife developed her strong missionary skills from this church and from her mother who was a great missionary in her own right. Mrs. Starr was angry with me as well. I guess it was out of concern for her baby girl. Whatever the case, as you could probably imagine I found it quite difficult to stay encouraged while dating my wife.

One of the bright spots however was attending church with my wife. I truly enjoyed going to church every Sunday. My Sunday school teacher was Sister Nicks. She was the former First Lady of the church. I was not attending the church when Reverend Nicks was alive, but I'd heard a lot of good things about him from everyone I'd talked to. The foundation that I received from Sister Nicks was unbelievable. She was the most learned lady I have ever met in church. I was baptized at St. James and we were married there as well.

GOD'S HAND CAN STOP TRAFFIC FOR YOU!

In 1989 I was involved in a major accident on I-75 South. I was returning from dropping my wife off at work. At this time my wife was employed at the IRS, in Downtown Detroit. I was on my way to work when a semi truck tried to change lanes and came over into my lane. When he did so, I looked over and noticed that the chain that holds the rear part of the truck to the front was loose and disconnected. So as he started to come over, he swung the rear part of his truck around and it pinned me up against the median wall in the middle of the freeway.

The first thing you have to understand is that driving in Michigan, during rush hour, is very dangerous. Everyone driving is either late for work or frustrated with how heavy traffic is this early in the morning. My wife has to be at work on or before the 7:00 am hour. So at the time of the accident it must have been 6:45 am or very close to it. The weather was slightly overcast with a small amount of rain falling. Everyone on the freeway was speeding, including me. We were driving at 60 to 65 miles per hour. The speed limit at that time was 55 miles per hour. So everyone was going a little fast. I was in the passing lane, because after all I was on my way to work as well.

After the accident came to a conclusion and I stopped shaking and calling on Jesus, I got out of my car and walked away without a scratch. I'll give you some understanding of how the accident ended. When I opened my car door to get out, there was a wall under the door. When I stood up to get out, a car that was traveling in the northbound direction or the opposite of the direction in which I was traveling, on the other side of the freeway, went under my car door. The person behind me on the freeway was not as blessed as I was. The driver of the 5.0 Mustang behind me was beheaded. At the time I was not aware of anyone being killed. I was attempting to get my senses in order.

When you are involved in something like this all you can say is "Thank you Jesus. Thank you Jesus." At first I thought I was dead and that this is what happens to you after you die. When you think about it, there is no way that I should have walked away from this accident without a scratch.

This caused me to understand that there was a calling on my life and that God was not finished molding me yet. You see since He knew us before time began, I know it's only a matter of time before I get back in touch with the Father.

Shortly after this accident, Rev. Trammer at St. James baptized me. I felt God calling me. I just did not know what He was calling me for. To fully understand the unbelievable deliverance I've just experienced takes spiritual discernment. During this accident I actually took my hands off the steering wheel and allowed God to steer me to a stop. Since it was raining slightly and the rear of that truck probably weighed twice as much as my car did, it made no sense to me to continue attempting to steer the vehicle. This is what I mean when I tell people that it was divine intervention that saved me.

I felt I owed God this much. So I became deeply involved with church and everything that was going on in it. I've attended church in the past, but this time there was a new passion, a fire that I can't explain. There was a desire in me to learn all there was about ministry and all that it entailed. Often when I speak to people about the incident I tell them that God took a bad situation and turned it around for my good.

Although I enjoyed attending St. James, this was not my first experience with attending church as you have already read. My wife seems to think that I need instruction in attending church, from time to time. Often when I would walk down an aisle to go to my seat she would look at me funny as if to say why are you going that way. It's true. Maybe I do not know proper etiquette, and maybe I am a little rough around the edges. But the desire is strong and sometimes I felt her staring at me was a slight discouragement. I remember getting angry with her about the way she would treat me. It was bad enough that I felt her family disliked me.

The church began looking for a new pastor. This caused me to become somewhat discouraged about attending St. James. The whole process started to leave a bad taste in my mouth concerning church politics. Every week we would have a new speaker, and you could look into the eyes of the ministers who were not speaking at the time, and see contempt for the person who was speaking. It was sort of like a competition. Everyone had their turn to impress the congregation.

St. James has a strange sort of church government system. The deacons and the people who have attended the church for a very long time had the responsibility of choosing the new pastor. This is something that I was not too familiar with. The church I attended as a child was not structured like this. It gave the church an atmosphere of business as usual. I don't know too much about the way a church is supposed to be run, but if you ask me, this way of managing the church takes away from the true purpose and intent of the Holy Ghost.

Shortly after that, the church seemed to fill up with homosexuals and people who were in need of some serious help. Excuse my French but I do not know another way to describe them. Don't misunderstand what I'm trying to say. The church is where this type of person needs to be to receive the help that is required. This caused my wife and I to decide to leave the church and look for a new church home. Not because of the people who were joining the church, but because of the atmosphere of business. This was a stench and that seemed to change the way we worshipped the Lord. Anything that would take away from my relationship with my Lord cannot be good. So this is why we decided to leave the church. At the time we left, we did not understand the true meaning of deliverance. But as we began to grow our faith we grabbed hold of the true meaning. I believe it was meant for us to leave that church and experience a true deliverance service. I believe the Lord was beginning to show us our ministry.

LIFE'S LESSONS

Over the years God has allowed me to see a lot of different situations. I was involved in some of them. I once attended this church that I thought was truly a blessed church. My wife and I attended this church for approximately two years. When things started to fall apart, I noticed that the pastor was getting sick a lot. However no one would tell my wife and me exactly what was wrong with him. Later on we discovered totally by accident that he was an alcoholic. While he was sick, I had accepted my calling to the ministry and was running services on the days he could not make it to service. The membership had almost completely left the church.

Most of the remaining members would sit and listen to me even though they knew I was not a preacher. As I began to study the Bible in preparation for the next sermon I would have to teach, I discovered that the Lord was providing me with the words to preach. There were ten faithful members left at the church. One of the members was an older lady who would give me motherly advice on what I should preach and how to do it.

Once again I noticed alcohol was playing a significant role in my life. Although I'm not an alcoholic, this demon has been a part of my life that I have not been able to get rid of. It's as if I've been drinking liquor for twenty years. Not only every person I meet but also now it's every situation I become involved in is saturated with this terrible concoction.

I remember asking this pastor, whose name I will not divulge at this time, to license me so that I would not be out of order. He would always say that he could not do it at that time. I never found out why he could not do it, when he was the one asking me to run the services. It was not my desire to stand before the people of this congregation every Sunday and tell them once again that "Your pastor is not able to be with you so I will be delivering the sermon today".

My wife and I would do the best we could to run the services as normally as we could considering the circumstances. We would bring inspirational hymns on cassette tapes along with a tape player. We would sing along with the tapes as we ushered in the Holy Spirit. We also collected offerings and took prayer requests. This lasted for about three months or so.

Prior to this pastor becoming ill, we had a revival service. I'll give you some idea of how popular this particular minister was. The revival service was one week long. Each service had about two hundred people in attendance. I sent for my Uncle Robert Popwell from Tennessee. He came with ten people from his church. This revival service was one of the largest I had ever been a part of. This service had to bring in at least one hundred thousand dollars in offerings. I mentioned this because of what happened next. Shortly after the revival ended, Michigan Consolidated Gas Company and Detroit Edison shut off the gas and lights. When my wife and I inquired about the balance to determine how much the church owed, we were shocked to discover the bill was an outrageous amount of $46,000. We could not believe this amount was accurate.

We inquired of the pastor and a few of the members and they verified the amount. We did not think anything was wrong because of the explanation we received from the pastor as to why the light and gas bill had not been paid. He informed us that there were two young men who were living in the upstairs apartment who did not pay their bills. So my wife and I never questioned the pastor about the unpaid bills. Now that I look back this should have given us some warning signs that something was wrong.

We were really taken advantage of while attending this church. When I think about some of the things that I have been through while attempting to be a good Christian, it's enough to make a person not want to be a part of the church. Then when I talk to people in the world about attending church, most of them mention things that have happened to me during my journey with Christ, as being the reason why they do not want to join the church. So you see a part of my Misery is my Ministry. The things that I have suffered in life are some of the things that I am capable of ministering to everyday people about. I believe that everything I have been through in life was for a reason. Most of the situations I have been involved in have given me an ability to respond to questions concerning certain specific situations.

In order to tell my story effectively I have had to discuss some painful situations so I want to take this time to ask God to forgive me. I do not want to put my mouth on any man of God. I realize that God allows people to go through things, so that His power may be made manifest in the earth, so that men might see His light and come crying, "What must I do to be saved?" Needless to say once we found out the pastor was an alcoholic, we decided to leave the church.

This was just one of the many things I have seen since accepting my calling to the ministry. I've learned over the years that everyone does not get a supernatural move of God when they are called into the ministry. Sometimes situations that a person finds his or herself in is usually testimony enough of God's purpose in his or her life.

Over and over again God has allowed me to be involved in leadership circumstances and situations ever since I have accepted my calling to the ministry. Once I visited a church where there was a young man who was a minister. He was an ex-drug user. He was familiar to me because I believe I sold him drugs when I was involved in that lifestyle. Seeing him gave me a renewed confidence in my calling to the ministry.

I recently had a dream. In the dream I was lying down and a man, or the enemy, was standing over me punching me in my chest. It wasn't an ordinary punch. It was as if he was reaching into my chest and ripping my heart right out between my ribs. I jumped up out of the bed immediately and began reading my Bible. I felt this was a sign of my impending death if I did not do what God was instructing me to do. Ever since I had this dream I have been doing everything I can to fulfill my calling in life. I am determined not to stop until God's purpose has been realized in my life.

A BOY HAS TO SEE A MAN TO LEARN HOW TO BE A MAN

You see I was never taught this principal, as simple as it may seem. Some of the things that most people take for granted in life were a struggle for me to grab hold of.

Most of the professional people that I see on television miss this simple equation in life. Without a father you can't truly understand how to be a man. A child needs to see a man in order for him to know how to be a man.

The examples I had in my life were drug dealers and low life individuals who did not try to get anything out of life. Please don't get me wrong. I'm not attempting to glorify this lifestyle. But the truth of the matter is that some of these guys have a very clear understanding of what it takes to be a man. It's like prisoners. They know more about life than the average professor in college knows. This is because these guys have learned the hard way to be men and how to take care of their responsibilities. What's unfortunate is that they have learned it too late. Most of them have either died or been arrested. And most of them unfortunately don't know Jesus. Oh, but HALLELUJAH! They will soon find out if I have anything to do with it.

Most people look down on prisoners, or people who have made mistakes in life. Remember a lot of the men of the Bible were prisoners. God recognized that there was an abundance of wisdom in the minds of prisoners. The Bible says that God takes the foolish things of the earth to confound the wise. When you find yourself locked up in prison, you discover a whole lot of quiet time for introspection and prayer. People who deal drugs are efficient at taking care of themselves. In life they would be excellent CPAs. Their math skills are impeccable.

They are masters of survival. So as a child you're drawn to the wisdom of the people who survive no matter what the economy looks like; in spite of what it may look like to the naked eye. When everyday people, law-abiding citizens, are laid off, because of a lack of work, drug dealers are able to continue to feed their children. They are still capable of taking care of themselves in spite of how bad times are. This is also symptomatic of the world we live in and the times. When most men that I know get laid off they turn up the bottle to get some solace for their self-esteem problems. Most men feel that they are the kings of their castle and when they can no longer provide for their castle it becomes a self-esteem problem for the breadwinner of the family.

So as a young man growing up in the ghetto or slums, drug dealers become heroes and the police become the bad guys. This is why young

African American men are more likely to fill up a jail cell rather than a university. People gravitate towards others with more knowledge than they have. And like me, most young black men grow-up in underprivileged households. Money was so tight in my house for years that a meal consisted of homemade biscuits and syrup.

I remember being so hungry that I would eat a spoon full of flour just so that my stomach would stop growling. We would often have cereal with no milk. So we would use water instead. This was pretty nasty but it was food. My stepfather would work and receive a paycheck but because of his alcohol addiction he did not take care of his household responsibilities, therefore we were without food a great deal of time.

I'm glad that the lessons I learned from him did not stick with me in life, because if I had followed his example I'd be an alcoholic right now. So you see the men who were in my immediate vicinity were all very bad examples to follow. This probably explains why I gravitated towards the street life rather than people in my home life.

MY PHYSICAL AND SPIRITUAL FATHER

My story is not that different from most people's story. I love the Lord probably more than anyone could imagine. This is probably due to the fact that I did not have a biological father in my life. I discovered at the tender age of 17 that Booker T. Moore was not my biological father. My brother and aunt told me during an argument one day. I subsequently discovered that my father was a Baptist minister and that he was the pastor of a church in my mother's neighborhood. His name was Henry Thomas (Vereen).

According to my mother, he wanted to take me from her but she would not let him. So I guess I can't be mad with him because he did attempt to do the best he could for me considering the circumstances.

In 1981 I returned to Georgia in an attempt to locate my father. I probably could have tried a little harder. The search ended unsuccessfully. However, I did get a chance to meet my great aunt and uncle. I am not hurt because of the lack of involvement of my father in my life. So I do not believe that this was a direct reason for my addiction to drugs. I only regret not being able to determine if he had Sickle Cell Anemia or not.

I started searching for him (HENRY THOMAS) by picking up the yellow pages and trying to call everyone with the same last name as my father. I was able to get in touch with someone in Michigan, who knew my family and gave me a number to call in Georgia. This in turn allowed me to get in touch with my father's sister. That is how I discovered where to go when I arrived in Georgia.

I went to Jacksonville, Florida to stay with my Aunt Alice (my mother's twin sister). We drove up to Georgia, during my brief stay with her, to see my grandmother and grandfather. This is when I took a trip to see my father. Needless to say, I was unsuccessful, so I returned to Michigan. Several years later I received a call from my father's sister in Georgia. She informed me that my father had died and that he left me some sort of liquor license. I never went to retrieve the license however. I felt whoever was doing the work in the place before he died should keep it.

After discovering this, I was pretty sad even though I never met him. Isn't that something? Even though I did not know him, it still made me sad to know that he was dead. You see even though I was not physically in contact with him, we were still connected spiritually.

Human nature is strange like that. We make attachments to things that we don't even know, although it may have been popular. My father might have been a wonderful man, but the fact is he never made an attempt to get in touch with me. It wasn't that hard for me to get in touch with him, so I know that he could have gotten in touch with me, if he had really wanted to.

I don't want to give the impression that I'm bitter, because I'm not. I would not change one aspect of my life.

I've learned that everything you go through in life is for a purpose. God has allowed you to see the problems and situations that you've seen for a reason. The Bible says that you "will reap in due season if you faint not". The actual scripture is Galatians 6:9. "And let us not be weary in well doing: for in due season we shall reap, if we faint not."

You see my mother had to leave Georgia. She did so that my ministry could go the way that it has begun to move. The Lord has allowed me to see how people act when they are living in the flesh. And how it is the anointing which destroys the yoke. I will no longer be entangled with the yoke of bondage in my life. This was done so that I could learn what not to do as a mature Christian.

MY DAMASCUS ROAD

I was fortunate in that I was never caught doing illegal activities. God caught me before officials did. One day on a dark street in River Rouge, the Lord allowed me to see someone get shot to death. This is what scared me straight. As I was becoming more and more involved in the drug underworld, I took a moment to step back and look at my life after this incident. And because the seed of faith was planted in my life at a young age, I was able to pray to God and ask Him to come in to my life and to save me from myself. Although God did not come when I wanted Him to, God was right on time. When I saw this young man die an untimely death, it wasn't long before I was almost taken away from here also. While standing in front of a restaurant selling drugs, two young men began shooting at my friend and me. I heard a bullet whistle past my head and hit the bulletproof glass right behind me. The glass from the window jumped out and hit me in the neck. Even though it is bulletproof it still chips when force is applied to it. Bulletproof glass is constructed to keep a bullet from penetrating through and causing bodily injury. Needless to say that was enough for me. I knew then that I could not continue to live like this.

After stealing from my mother for the last time, she evicted me. I literally had nowhere to go. The Ecorse, River Rouge, Detroit and State of Michigan Police Agencies raided the house I was staying in one week earlier. I escaped just before the raid began. Therefore I had nowhere to go. So I slept in a homeless shelter for one night. While I was there I witnessed big giant rats running through the room where the mattresses were. There was a large room with mattresses on the floor. I did not want to live my life sleeping in the same room with giant rats. The next day I signed myself into a rehabilitation hospital. This was not an easy task. You had to pretend to be suicidal before they would take you in the hospital. Because at this time all of the hospitals were full of people addicted to crack. Alone in that hospital I learned more about myself than all of my years living in River Rouge, Michigan.

After 45 days I was told that I could no longer stay there. However at this point I still felt that I was not ready to go back to the same neighborhood I had just come out of. So I told the social worker at the hospital that I had nowhere to go. She signed me up for a group home. I lived there for one year. After living with mentally insane people for one year I came to the reality that I was better than what people labeled me as. All my life friends and family told me that I would never amount to anything and that I was destined for failure. Well I'm here to tell you that you don't have to live the way people say you should. God has a plan for your life. When He says it's time for you to move that's when you move. When I felt that it was time for me to leave, I signed up for some college courses at Wayne County Community College. I earned an "A" in every course I took. Here I learned that I was worth more than I had been led to believe. After being told that I had to leave the group home, I moved back in to my mother's house. I didn't do this until I wrote her an exhaustive letter explaining how much I loved and appreciated her for what she had done for me. When she kicked me out of her house, it caused me to realize my potential. Suddenly I knew that I was worth more than what I had been told.

After completing one semester of college courses, I realized that I was living with my mother once again and not contributing to the household. So I went out and got a job. This is where a part of my story makes a significant change. I met my wife. I actually went to a house to buy some illegal insurance for a friend of mine. This house happened to be across the street from my wife's house.

She came over to the house while I was there. We made an immediate connection. The connection was so strong that when I got back in the car with my friends, my brother asked me, "Who was that girl?" I answered, "That's going to be my wife. Leave her alone." From that point on we have been inseparable.

I thank and praise God for the victory today. If it had not been for His grace and mercy I could still be living in a homeless shelter. So now when I hear someone saying that they wish they could stop using drugs or stop smoking or drinking, I just say to them that God is able. If you put God first He will rebuke the devourer for your sake.

MY MISERY IS MY MINISTRY!

My life has been filled with pain and bumps and curves in the road. And many people know that when you drive around a curve, the inertia from the curve causes your body to lean from one side to the other. This is how I feel that my life has gone. First I started out leaning on the side of God. I went to the sunshine band with my friends when I was little. Then when I got older I started leaning the other way when I was introduced to smoking weed, and the life of sin, where I thought that my only reason for being here was to satisfy the lusts of the flesh. One thing about inertia is that whenever it causes you to lean you always come back to center. Hallelujah! I thank God for the center. Because it's in the center that we realize it's just a curve. It's in the center that we know that trouble won't last always. Thank you Jesus for the center.

FINDING MY NICHE

From the age of fourteen years old, I've worked for approximately twenty different employers. Every one of them taught me a different lesson about life. Some taught me the value of money, and others taught me how to make it without money. Most of the people I worked for in Michigan, I'm sad to say were racists. I don't want anyone to misunderstand what I'm saying. These individuals don't think they're doing anything wrong. As a matter of fact, if you say that they are racists, they claim reverse discrimination immediately, as if that's the automatic answer to your accusation. So I've discovered that most African Americans prefer not to say anything as opposed to opening the proverbial can of worms. Somehow they have made us ashamed of calling things the way they are. All of my life I have been taught to call a bird, a bird and a fish, a fish. In other words I only know how to call things the way I see them. I feel that the main problem in America is that African Americans have become afraid to say what they feel.

I can't remember how many times I've been walking to my car, and some white person would see me and lock their car door, as if because I'm a black man that automatically means I'm a thief, or a person with bad intentions in mind. I believe that if we begin to tell people that this bothers us, they will think twice before they do it again.

I once worked for a grocery store and because of my dedication and hard work unto the Lord, they considered me for a management job. However when the store got a new manager, who happened to be white, all of a sudden they decided to hire three new white managers and not hire me as a manager. Now you have to understand that before they hired this new person to manage the store, they were using me as a manager and not paying me comparable pay. In other words I was still receiving stock boy pay and doing managerial work. When I asked them about this, they quickly labeled me as a troublemaker, and for whatever reason I was no longer considered for the job.

Because of my Christianity, I just move on and say that it wasn't my time yet. Out of the twenty jobs that I've had, five of them offered me an opportunity for management. All five hired a white guy who was less qualified, and not as hard a worker as I was, instead of hiring me. This includes the job that I am currently working. However I have decided to do something about it this time. Let us get a clear understanding of what I am saying. When they hired these managers every one of them had to come to me and ask me how to do something that is concerning their job. Now if I have to tell them how to do the job, wouldn't it be more sensible to make me a manager and not have to worry about me knowing how to do the job?

Now that I realize that these jobs are not my source, I'm no longer worried about losing my job. No longer will I stand by and allow people to treat me any kind of way. The Lord is my provider, and just as He feeds the birds of the air surely He will not allow me to starve, as long as I continue to serve him. And as long as I continue to pay my tithes and be faithful to the call that is on my life, I know that GOD will never leave me nor forsake me. This is a principal that I have not always been comfortable with. But since I've come back from Bishop T. D. Jakes' Mega Fest Conference, I have a new revelation of God's plan for my life.

YOU FIT THE DESCRIPTION

The Bible says that, "My people perish for lack of knowledge". I do not want us ever to forget the struggle and what it has meant to us for some forty years now.

While training for a new coating line on my job, I was allowed to go home for lunch. After finishing lunch and while I was returning to the training location, I noticed that there was a Chevrolet van following me at a very slow rate of speed. While traveling on Outer Drive, the van drove very slowly maintaining a slight distance behind me. I did not pay the van much attention. I continued to return to the Stinson Center. This is the place where our training took place. When I pulled into the parking lot and prepared to exit my vehicle, five unmarked cars pulled into the parking lot and surrounded my van. Very quickly I realized that they were police and that something was very wrong.

I still remember to this day the one older Caucasian officer who seemed to be in charge as they pulled me out of my car and began searching me.

He pulled out his handgun and pointed it at my nose and told me to shut up and to put my hands up in the air. I began to explain to these gentlemen, who were being anything but gentleman at the time, that whoever they were looking for was getting away, and that I was not guilty of doing anything, because this was my job and that I was returning from lunch. At this time the older gentleman began to manhandle me and yell that I was the guy he was looking for.

Well, I guess that by this time you are probably saying to yourself, "What did he do?" That is the ironic part of all of this. Because it turns out that after they handcuffed me and took me from my job like a common criminal, they had the wrong guy. Apparently I fit the description.

At the time of this incident, I was living with my sister-in-law. The individual they were looking for was an ex-boyfriend of my sister-in-law. What description did I fit? Apparently, I fit the description of a common criminal, a drug addict, a felon, or even worse, perhaps a murderer. What did I do to deserve this label? Being born an African American and living in the City of Detroit? Or was it because I was in the vicinity and someone had to be detained to justify the effort? When I saw a picture of the guy they said I was, he did not look anything like me. The guy had a light complexion and was bald with facial hair.

I have begun to change that image. Now I want the very (IMOGIDA) of Christ. (Genesis 1:27) "So God created man in his own image, in the image of God created he him, male and female created he them." This is why I have written this book to let people know that all African American males are not criminals who fit the description. Some of us fit a different description. God has created us in His image. Why should I walk around with a hat pulled down over my face as if I'm afraid to show myself, for fear of some sort of persecution? No, I'm proud of who I am. I'm proud to be a member of the body of Christ, and I'm also proud to be a member of the International Gospel Center, in Ecorse, Michigan.

Never again will I walk around with my head hanging down. I've learned as a child of the highest God not to be ashamed of anything. The Bible says that if we are ashamed of Christ, He will be ashamed of us as He makes intercession for us before the Father.

THE ANOINTING

My life now is much different from then. I am currently a member of the International Gospel Center of Ecorse, Michigan, where my Pastor is Rev. Marvin N. Miles. Pastor Miles has a real anointing on his life. My wife joined the ministry first. I was still going through my desert.

After being ordained as an Elder at the Mt. Carmel Full Gospel Assembly Non-Denominational Church. God sent me into the wilderness for several years. Now that I have received a word from the Lord, our ministry can begin.

I found out that God had to clean some things out of me before he would allow me to fulfill my calling in Christ.

I used to smoke one pack of cigarettes a day. God took that away while I was in my desert. An unforgiving spirit was holding me captive as well. The Lord delivered me from a lot of things while I was in my desert. But the most important thing that occurred for me while I was in the desert was my ministry was born.

Moore Outreach Ministry was birthed while I was in my desert. God has shown me that by fasting and prayer, the secrets of God can be revealed. In the Bible when Moses returned from the Mountain of Sinai, He asked the children of Israel "Who is on the Lord's side?" (Exodus 32:26) Whose report will you believe? I'm going to believe the report of the Lord.

God sent me into the wilderness for seven years. After GOD ordained me, I came under tremendous attack by the enemy. It wasn't until I joined the International Gospel Center, that I realized what was happening to me. My Pastor called me out one day, not knowing who I was, and referred to me as Man of God. When he did that I knew that God was still working in my life. He confirmed something that was told to me at Mega Fest. Bishop T.D. Jakes said that I was meant for much more than what the enemy was trying to tell me.

Pastor Miles said to me that things would start to flow more abundantly in my life than I could have ever imagined, spiritually, wealth, and my health. That is when I knew that my book was right on time.

So as I begin this journey into the hedges and highways, to help deliver and heal a hurting land I ask that you would pray for me. Pray that when I've done all that I can do to stand that I would continue to stand. Pray my strength in the Lord. Because it's in God we live, and breathe and have our very being. Remember that we can do all things through Christ who strengthens us as long as we keep our eyes on the prize for the high calling, which is in Christ Jesus. Thank you for listening and stay tuned for more books to be published by me as I start this new writing career.

GOD'S COUNSEL

I learned to lean on the unchanging hand of God at an early age. I would cry out to God, "Why me, oh Lord? Why did I have to be born with this terrible disease?" The Lord would minister to me while I was in pain. As a little child I did not realize what it was. I would think I was a little crazy, so I never told anyone that I was hearing voices in my head. I know now it was the Lord. God showed me that sin is the reason for my disease. And the blood of Jesus is able to take away the sin of the world.

Now I want to use this opportunity to help someone else make it through his or her pain, and let him or her know that when you think that you're hurting there's always someone who's hurting more than you and that your misery is your ministry. God has a plan for you in your life. He's teaching you something in this painful part of your life. As you grow please realize that your pain is only temporary. God is teaching you how to change what you're looking at although you can't change how you feel. God is able to heal you of your pain.

The Lord provides holy counsel to you. The problem is that most people on this earth do not attend church. So they do not know that God is a counselor, that He is a Provider and a Healer. When people suffer from the everyday repetitive actions of the God of this world they need to know JESUS. They need to receive counsel from the Lord, so that they will know that they can make it, and that trouble and pain don't last always.

WHOSE REPORT
WILL YOU BELIEVE?

My story is not much different than most people's story. However there is one big difference. I was born with a debilitating illness, which I've learned through the help of my Lord and Savior Jesus Christ to overcome.

You see, the Bible says that we are more than conquerors; we're overcomers. I have learned to overcome some things that I'm faced with on a daily basis. I was once told that I would not live to be 21 years old. A doctor told me this as well as a neighborhood mother. Well I'm here to tell you that they were wrong. This doctor's visit was in the early 1970's. I don't remember the exact date. That shows you how much I considered what he said. I realized at an early age that my way out of this problem was to go through it. It was not going away and I could not get around it. But when I heard that from this devil I told him that he was a liar and that I am the righteousness of God in Christ Jesus. I could do all things through Christ that strengthens me. No man can tell me when I am going to die. Man did not have the power to create me so in turn man cannot tell me when it is over. Since I've been born again I have discovered a whole new attitude about life. I'm not worried or frightened about death anymore. Death is the ultimate gain of this journey that we are all traveling. The question becomes what will you do with this time the Lord has blessed you with. You can choose to be a blessing while you're here or you can choose to be a curse. What is your choice?

PURPOSE!

What was my purpose? My answer came from a VHS tape by Dr. Myles Munroe. It helped me to understand that I had a purpose.

Even though I knew I had a purpose, it didn't mean that I understood it. It has taken me almost forty-three years to discover what my purpose is.

While growing up I found myself constantly in charge. If I wasn't in charge of my brothers and sisters, I was in charge of some activity that my friends were involved in. Through this I've learned some very valuable leadership skills. My mother was always busy doing something so therefore I was left to watch the family while she did other things, like working or shopping or something. And every job that I have ever worked has always turned into training for a supervisory position. Even sinners who are lost can recognize my natural leadership abilities. This has never been my choice in life, but because I have been so blessed by God, that I have been given a visionary gift which gives me the ability to see people in their weaknesses and to be able to help them. These are leadership gifts directly from God. I have always been told that I was very mature for my age. The old people would say that it was as if I had been here before. I don't believe in that however. These blessings come from God. The Bible says "Every good gift and every perfect gift is from above, and cometh down from the Father of lights, with who is no variableness, neither shadow of turning." (James 1:17) So you see I am a born leader.

Believing my book was finish I started to get it published. Although the story wasn't finished yet.

THE RESURRECTION!

In the year of 2009 I became gravely ill. My wife stated that when she Looked at me she started to think about what suit I should were in my Casket. I had caught an infection and because I did not go to the hospital right away, I became ischemic and my blood pressure dropped to 40 over 20. Therefore I could not have pain killers or certain medications that might cause a person's blood pressure to drop. I did not understand what was going on with me. I have been sick before and this felt like I was having a typical crisis. When the Emergency room Doctor came back in my room and said he wanted to put a needle in my chest right under my right collar bone, then I began to get worried.

I had never had a needle placed in that area before. Then the Doctor said You will be admitted to the hospital because you are to sick to go home. When I arrived at the main hospital located on Grand Blvd. in the city of Detroit, and taken directly up to the intensive care unit. This is when

I began to worry about my well being. There was a nurse position in my room continuously. Fifteen Doctors and nurses were in my room at one time, they told me they were going to place a tube down my throat to help me breathe. This is when I became unconscious for several days.

While I was unconscious my Pastor and several members of my church Came to visit me in the ICU. The only thing I can remember while I was Unconscious was my Pastor whispering in my ear to come back. He said it is not your time to die. Unbeknown to me at the time I was literally on my death bed. My blood pressure was so low that they could not give me anything to relieve the pain. So the Doctor's decided to put me in a medical induced coma, for my own good. While unconscious several procedures were performed on me. I had all of my blood drained and replaced with new blood. I never new this was possible, but I must commend the Doctor's for their efforts. GOD already had my situation under control. Never once did I fear for my life during all that I was going thru. I knew the LORD would take care of me. I didn't have no doubt.

My Doctors were so concerned about me that even after I awake from my coma I was kept in ICU for an additional week. My wife was so worried about me that she was trying to see what suit she would get for me at my funeral. When I awoke from my coma I noticed that the white's of my eyes were dark red in color It frightened me when I saw my eyes. We have been taught that the devil is red with a pitch fork. So you can imagine what was going thru my mind as I gazed upon my eyes.

It really impressed me to see my Pastor come in my room to talk with me and have prayer with me. My Pastor is a very busy man and for him to take time out of his schedule to come and see me, was unheard of. But I commend my Pastor for being a Pastor first, even though he is a busy man he is never to busy for his flock that GOD has given him charge over. Sometimes we get so tied up in the business of the church, that we sometimes forget what our true calling is. This has never been Pastor Marvin Miles problem. Sometimes I feel that he is over-worked. For example every Sunday at the end of service, even though he is tired and sweaty from preaching, Pastor takes time out to lay hands on anyone who stands in need of prayer. I must confess that this does cause me some concern. Thru the years of my studying the Word of GOD, I've learned that demons can jump off people and land on you as you pray.

With the anointing that my Pastor is operating under he can not afford something like that happening to him. He is so in touch with the holy spirit that he called me back from the dead. Now if this wasn't GOD'S will it would have never happen. That's how a person can tell if he or she is following the right ministry or not. Does your pastor hear from GOD? Or is he following his own agenda. Plan and purpose are so important when called to the ministry. That's why it has taken me so long to come into my purpose within the Body of Christ. I had to wait until I was absolutely sure that it was GOD calling me to do what I do. Make no mistake GOD is no respecter of person's, whatever he has for me, he could also have for you.

My story does not end here however, One year after my brush with death I found myself in the hospital again. This time the Doctor's said that my kidney's failed. I could not believe what was happening to me. To make things worst, I had to call and ambulance to take me to the hospital. They informed me that they could only take me to one of two hospitals in the area, Henry Ford in Wyandotte or Oakwood hospital in Dearborn. I have never been to either one of these hospitals before. Upon arrival by ambulance to Wyandotte hospital, I noticed right away that they were not in any hurry to treat me for my ailments. I was vomiting with diarrhea for three days and in severe pain. It took two hours for a doctor to come in my room and examine me, and then I was forced to stay in the emergency room for thirty hours after receiving treatment. The worst part of the visit was after two medically qualified doctors wrote orders for my treatment in my chart, two nurses came on duty at 7:00am the next morning and refused to follow those orders. They stated that hospital policy did not allow them to treat me the way the doctors orders instructed them too. So I asked to see a copy of the hospital policy with that statement on it. After promising to give me a copy of the statement they avoided me and never gave me a copy of the policy. Eventually I asked to be transferred to the main hospital downtown where I was treated according to my ailment and not the color of my skin.

I started writing this book five years ago, and I could not figure out why I could never publish the writing. Now I know it was because GOD was not Finish with me yet. I'm not saying that GOD caused me to get sick.

I am saying that GOD knew that my full testimony was not ready to be heard yet. He knew that there was a greater blessing waiting to be heard by the masses. And that someone could really be delivered by a LAZARUS testimony.

The saints at my church call me LAZARUS now, because I can truly say that I have been raised from the dead. Make no mistake I am not claiming to be the second coming of CHRIST. But what I am hear to do is testify to the mighty power of GOD. So many saints today are so fixed on the fact that CHRIST died for them, and only a handful are willing to say that he lives. Well I am here to tell you that CHRIST got up after dying for our sins. And he got up with all power in his hands. He conquered death and sickness when he died. So we would not have to suffer or be afraid of it anymore. When he rose on the third day, he came up with power over these things. So although I may be sick I know that my redeemer lives. As he rose to heaven he left us with the Holy Spirit who is our comforter. So make no mistake GOD is my redeemer, he's my healer, he's my way maker, and he alone is the reason I live. I live to serve him in whatever capacity he chooses, however he see's fit to use me, I'm available. So until we meet again, if it's on the pages of a book or in person. May the LORD watch between me and thee.